If you are wise enough you will make a book out of these stories from Ayuuḵhl Nisg̱a'a and pass on, from generation to generation, the wisdom the elders passed to me. I did not invent these stories. They come from up and down the Nass River and tell how the Nisg̱a'a live. When my time comes to leave this world, you'll have these stories to tell.

SIM'OOGIT G̱ADEEĹIBIM HAYATSKW
CHIEF RUFUS WATTS

Chief Israel Sgat'iin

NISGA'A

People of the Nass River

FOREWORD BY THOMAS R. BERGER
INTRODUCTION BY FRANK CALDER

DOUGLAS & McINTYRE
VANCOUVER/TORONTO

NISGA'A TRIBAL COUNCIL
GITLAKDAMIKS

Dedicated to the People of the Nisga'a Nation
Past — Present — Future

NISGA'A TRIBAL COUNCIL
PO Box 231
New Aiyansh, British Columbia
V0J 1A0

DOUGLAS & McINTYRE LTD.
1615 Venables Street
Vancouver, British Columbia
V5L 2H1

Canadian Cataloguing in Publication Data

Main entry under title:
Nisga'a : people of the Nass River

Co-published by the Nisga'a Tribal Council.
ISBN 1-55054-128-5

1. Niska Indians.
2. Indians of North America — British Columbia — Nass River Region.
I. Nishga Tribal Council.
E99.N734N58 1993   971.1'1   093-091773-1

Editor: Alex Rose

Editorial Committee:
Esther Adams
Joseph Gosnell Sr.
Nelson Leeson
Alvin McKay
John A. Mackenzie
Rod Robinson
Edmond Wright

Book Design: Jim Skipp
Photography: Gary Fiegehen
Printed in Canada by H. MacDonald Printing

End sheets: Chief Gideon Minee'eskw and wife Agnes on Lisims, the Nass River

Gwinahaa Pts'aan of Chief Aҳdiimin'aajaҳ

‹ FOREWORD ›

by Thomas R. Berger

The issue of aboriginal rights is the oldest question of human rights in Canada. At the same time it is also the most recent, for it is only in the last two decades that it has entered our consciousness and our political bloodstream. It began centuries ago with the white occupation of a continent already inhabited by another race, a race with its own cultures, its own languages, its own institutions and its own way of life.

Today the members of that race are advancing claims to the lands they once occupied—and in many cases still occupy—and calling for the right to self-determination and self-government. These claims give rise to fundamental issues that are somehow bound up with what happened long ago and are an unresolved and unfinished part of Canadian history.

Aboriginal rights are simply the rights to which native peoples are entitled because they are the original peoples of Canada. Until recently, the idea of aboriginal rights seemed irrelevant to Canadian concerns. But during the 1970s we began to realize that aboriginal rights are the axis around which our relations with aboriginal peoples revolve.

To recognize aboriginal rights is to understand the truth of our own history, while, for the aboriginal peoples, such recognition is the means by which they may achieve a distinct and contemporary place in Canadian life.

The history of white-native relations in Canada may be epitomized in the history of relations between whites and Indians in British Columbia. Here the aboriginal protest over the loss of their lands has been more audible than elsewhere, and the Indian land question has agitated the province for more than a century.

The Nisga'a Indians have been pioneers in establishing aboriginal rights—not only for themselves—but for aboriginal people throughout Canada and the world. It is serendipitous that this book should appear in this the twentieth anniversary year of the Calder case (named for Frank Calder, President of the Nisga'a Tribal Council at the time), which was a turning point in white-aboriginal relations in this country. For the Nisga'a, their struggle did not begin with that case, but its outcome was instrumental in fundamentally altering Canada's policy on aboriginal rights.

The story of the Nisga'a illustrates the quest of all Canadian Indians for legal recognition of their aboriginal rights. It takes us back to the beginnings of European colonization of North America, and brings us forward to the very centre of the present conflict over land claims, aboriginal self-determination and the concept of aboriginal government.

In November 1971, chiefs of the four villages in the Nass valley, together with village elders wearing their traditional sashes, travelled to Ottawa for the hearing of their case in the Supreme Court of Canada. For five days, seven judges heard the argument of the appeal. Then they reserved their decision for fourteen months.

Mr. Justice Wilfred Judson, speaking for three judges, found that the Nisga'a, before the coming of the white man, had aboriginal title, a title recognized under English law. But, he went on to say, this title had been extinguished by pre-Confederation enactments of the old colony of British Columbia. Mr. Justice Emmett Hall, speaking for three judges, found that the Nisga'a, before the coming of the white man, had aboriginal title, that it had never been lawfully extinguished, and that this title could be asserted even today.

On this reckoning, the court was tied. The seventh judge dismissed the case on a technicality but did not address the question of aboriginal title. What was significant for aboriginal rights was that all of the six judges who had addressed the main question supported the view that English law, in force in British Columbia when colonization began, had recognized Indian title to the land.

Mr. Justice Judson, in describing the nature of Indian title, concluded: "The fact is that when the settlers came the Indians were there, organized in societies and occupying the land as their forefathers had done for centuries. This is what Indian title means. What they are asserting in this action is that they had a right to continue to live on their lands as their forefathers had lived and that this right has never been lawfully extinguished."

He went on to hold that the old pre-Confederation colony of British Columbia had effectively extinguished the aboriginal title of the Nisga'a.

Mr. Justice Hall, who with two of his colleagues was prepared to uphold the Nisga'a claim, urged that the court should adopt a contemporary view and not be bound by past and mistaken notions about Indians and Indian culture. He said: "What emerges from the . . . evidence is that the Nishgas [common spelling at the time] in fact are and were from time immemorial a distinctive cultural entity with concepts of ownership indigenous to their culture and capable of articulation under the common law, having 'developed their cultures to higher peaks in many respects than in any other part of the continent north of Mexico.' "

He held that the Nisga'a title could be asserted today. No matter that the province would be faced with innumerable legal tangles. What was right was right.

The Supreme Court's judgement, although it was not handed down until February 1973, came at a propitious moment. The election of 1972 had returned the Liberals to power, but as a minority government. To remain in office, the Liberals depended on the goodwill of the opposition parties. So the question of aboriginal title was catapulted into the political arena.

In Parliament, both the Conservatives and the New Democrats insisted that the federal government must recognize its obligation to settle native claims. The all-party Standing Committee on Indian and Northern Affairs passed a motion that approved the principle that a settlement of native claims should be made in regions where treaties had not already extinguished aboriginal title. On August 8, 1973, Jean Chrétien, then Minister of Indian Affairs, announced that the federal government intended to settle the claims, beginning a process that continues to this day.

In North and South America there are 50 million native people, almost everywhere dispossessed, everywhere poor, everywhere powerless. In the past they refused to be exterminated; today they will not be assimilated. They insist that we must address the issues that have pursued us since Columbus set foot in the New World. In Canada this can be achieved through a fair settlement of native claims. The settlement of these claims may, therefore, be important to men and women in many countries, a contribution to the legal and political order of enormous use to humanity, one the Nisga'a will have done much to secure.

Chief Israel Sgat'iin's ceremonial mask

◄ INTRODUCTION ►

by Frank Calder

We are Nisga'a—the people who live in the Nass River valley of northwestern British Columbia and claim it as our territory. We intend to live here in the Nass forever.

The river and its watershed—from glacial headwaters to Pacific estuary—provided the food, fur, tools, plants, medicine, timber and fuel that enabled us to develop one of the most sophisticated cultures in North America.

Since the last great Ice Age we travelled, fished and settled along all 380 kilometres of the river and its tributaries. In Ayuukhl Nisga'a—our ancient oral code—there are many stories describing the river and its special places. In modern times, the river flooded three times—in 1917, 1936 and 1960. After the 1960 flood we moved our village of Gitlakdamiks to higher ground.

Despite the travesty of cut-and-run logging and the poisons that leach from abandoned mines, the Nass is still a place of pristine alpine beauty, unpolluted air, ancient forests and dramatic landscapes of volcanic lava and glaciers.

Out on the Pacific coast, fjords knife into a long line of jagged mountain peaks, where a vast, forested landscape drapes itself over the Coast Range. A sometimes harsh climate is moderated by warm winds and clouds that scud across the Pacific Ocean, bringing heavy rain and snow.

Our homeland—all 24,862 square kilometres of it —straddles a spectacular route to Yukon and Alaska from Canada and northward to the glacier-fed lakes of Meziadin and Bowser. From the Skeena Mountains in the northeast to the intersection of the Alaska Panhandle and the B.C. coast, this is Nisga'a land.

The Nass supports all five species of Pacific salmon, the most important currency we have ever known. Rich salmon runs were harvested in a manner that allowed us to build our villages and develop a far-flung trading empire that reached deep into the Interior and ranged up and down the coast.

Besides salmon and steelhead, the Nass is home to the oolichan, a finger-sized member of the smelt family which is a mainstay of our culture and an historic staple of Nisga'a trade. In earlier times we shared our oolichan grounds with other tribes hungry after long winters. Oolichan are also known as "candlefish" because when dried, they retain enough oil to burn like a candle. We catch tonnes of the tiny fish every year near Fishery Bay.

With the oolichan comes its predators: the sea lions, seals, porpoises, Orca whales, eagles and flocks of gulls as thick as a snow blizzard.

Moving inland, giant hemlock, cedar and sitka spruce forests gradually change to spruce, lodgepole and jack pine and balsam forests, while stands of cottonwood cloak the valley floor.

For more than 10,000 years, we have thrived in this land, organizing ourselves into four clans—Gisk'ahaast (Killer Whale), Laxgibuu (Wolf), Ganada (Raven) and Laxsgiik (Eagle).

We still hunt, fish and trap. But today we are also lawyers, administrators, politicians, priests, teachers, linguists, loggers, commercial fishermen, carvers, dancers, nurses, architects, technicians and business people.

Our population now numbers about 6,000. About 2,500 people live in the Nisga'a villages of Gingolx (Kincolith), Lakalzap (Greenville), Gitwinksihlkw (Canyon City) and Gitlakdamiks (New Aiyansh). Another 3,500 live elsewhere in Canada and around the world.

At present, we are the only First Nation in B.C. formally negotiating land claims with the federal and provincial governments. The Nisga'a Land Question will be settled. Of that we are certain. We are prepared to do whatever is necessary to bring this about. Our elders are teaching us to look inside to find the strength and purity we need. Our young people are coming back from the cities to consult with our elders and to learn from them. They are bringing back home the skills and education we will need to build a new economy in the Nass. We are ready and poised for a new era for the Nisga'a Nation.

Devastated by smallpox, influenza and other diseases brought by Europeans, our ancestors were torn from their homes, exiled to reserves, forbidden to speak the Nisga'a language and practise our own beliefs. In short, we have been subjected to a system of cultural genocide for the past 130 years.

But we have survived to become, in the final days of this century, a powerful symbol of rebirth and renewal for many of the First Nations of the world.

In these pages we reaffirm title to our land and offer a contemporary portrait of our people accompanied by quotes from our oral history—Ayuukhl Nisga'a.

Look at our faces. We are survivors. We have a story to tell.

Chief Ksdiyaawak and family, 1903

NISGA'A NATION

TRADITIONAL TERRITORY

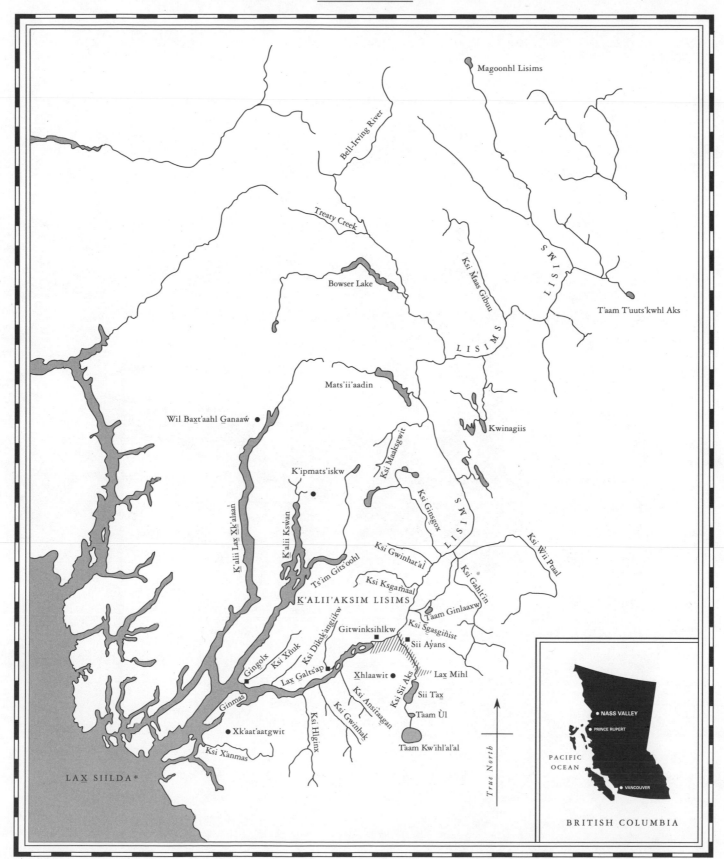

Magoonhl Lisims

Bell-Irving River

Treaty Creek

Ksi Maas Gibuu

S W I S T

L I S I M S

T'aam T'uuts'kwhl Aks

Bowser Lake

Mats'ii'aadin

Kwinagiis

Wil Baxt'aahl Ganaaẃ •

K'ipmats'iskw

Ksi Maaksgwit

S W I S T

L I S I M S

Ksi Ginsgox

K'alii Lax Xk'alaaṅ

K'alii Kswan

Ksi Gwinhat'al

Ksi W'ii Ptaal

Ts'im Gits'oohl

Ksi Ksgamaal

Ksi Gahlt'in

K'ALII'AKSIM LISIMS

T'aam Ginlaaxẃ

Gingolx

Ksi Xhuk

Ksi Diksk'angiikw

Ksi Sgasgiṅist

Gitwinksihlkw ■

Sii Ayans ■

Gingolx ●

Lax Galts'ap ■

Xhlaawit ●

Lax Mihl

Ginmas

Ksi Ans'iaangan

Ksi Sii Aks

Sii Tax

Ksi Gwinhak

T'aam Ùl

Xk'aat'aatgwit ●

Ksi Hlginx

T'aam Kw'ihl'al'al

Ksi X'anmas

True North

LAX SIILDA*

BRITISH COLUMBIA

NASS VALLEY

PRINCE RUPERT

PACIFIC
OCEAN

VANCOUVER

*All Nisga'a names, common spelling at the time   ■ Nisga'a villages   ● Sacred mountains   ///// Lava beds   Note: Map is representational, not to scale

Walking slowly, but with great purpose, Nisga'a Elder Bert McKay navigates his way along the muddy gravel road that winds through Gitlakdamiks (New Aiyansh) to the village school.

On a bright spring day, stacks of cumulous cloud loaded with Pacific rain press against Xhlaawit (Vetter Peak) and the other knife-edged mountains of the Boundary Range that ring this volcanic valley, as if to encircle the Nisga'a world.

Bert is one of a team working to preserve the Ayuukhl Nisga'a—the ancient code of laws and customs. They have dedicated themselves to researching this massive body of work, translating and transferring the stories told by Nisga'a elders first to paper and now to computer disc.

Ayuukhl Nisga'a is primarily the record of one Nation, its mythology and its image of the world. It is Nisga'a history as told by the Nisga'a themselves: the creation of the world, the flood, the volcano, the legends behind local topography, the founding of the great families and their crests, the mystical feats of warriors, shamans and spirit beings.

Besides being a storehouse of mythic stories, Ayuukhl Nisga'a is also a sophisticated set of laws that establishes and defines Nisga'a institutions, as well as a code of conduct. Under the code, every Nisga'a belongs to a tribe and a wilp or house which owns its songs, crests, dances, stories and territory. There are now about 60 wilps which own and manage 40 ango'oskws (family territories) comprising Nisga'a land.

All these rights are handed down through matrilineal succession in a ceremony known as the Settlement Feast. Like a deed in a land registry office, the Settlement Feast is a formal registration of title and ownership.

Totally oral, the stories of Ayuukhl Nisga'a retain a solid base in ritual and are enlivened with each performance—there is no fixed or authoritative version; they change in nuance. Often accompanied by songs and dances, they scintillate with humanity, life and the power of faith and imagination. And while they resurrect a vanished world, they are deliberately and accurately historical.

This wisdom is the province of those steeped in the tradition of the tribe and dates to a distant time.

Today, Bert tells an adaawak or story from the code to another generation of Nisga'a—a class of Grade 10 students.

Settling into a chair at the front of the classroom, Bert begins to speak in his mother tongue—Nisga'a. Words, whole phrases, are repeated with the primacy of poetry.

Many years ago, before the logging road pushed up from Terrace, Bert left the reserve by boat, sailing downriver to Gingolx and then down the coast to Victoria where he studied to be a teacher. After receiving his teaching diploma in 1950, he moved to Alert Bay on the northern tip of Vancouver Island where he taught for four years. In 1954 Bert returned to Lakalzap, as that community's first college-educated Nisga'a teacher, to work in a tiny, two-room school.

Above: Kingfisher mask

Conditions were so bad, Bert recalls, that he and other members of the newly-formed Nisga'a Tribal Council made education their first priority, pressing governments so that "we could control and manage our own education."

Today, School District 92 (Nisga'a), created in 1977, is the first native-run school district in Canada, a landmark of cross-cultural development. There are elementary schools in all four villages and a fine cedar and lava rock-faced secondary school at Gitlakdamiks.

The schools are bilingual and bicultural, with lessons in the Nisga'a language for both native students and non-natives from the logging community of Nass Camp. The school system now sends growing numbers of students on to university.

The Nisga'a language is compulsory from kindergarten to Grade 7 and an elective for university-bound students in Grades 8 to 12. It is an accredited second language at B.C. universities and colleges.

The school system is a triumph for a nation that feared for its survival in the early part of this century when a misguided government decided to integrate natives into Canadian society by putting them in boarding homes away from the influence of their families.

"As these people came back from the residential schools, the elders realized there was something wrong with them," says Bert, who was sent to an Anglican residential school in Alert Bay at the age of nine.

"They were neither white nor Nisga'a. They were in between, in sort of a vacuum. One thing was most noticeable—they had forgotten their language. There is no more effective way to undermine a culture than to destroy its language. In residential schools, our children were made to feel ashamed of being Indian."

A turning point came in the mid-1950s when supplies for an upcoming school year arrived in a shipment from the federal government.

"Six boxes came from Ottawa," Bert says recalling the incident that galvanized Nisga'a resolve for educational autonomy. "We opened them. Two boxes contained discarded textbooks from an Ontario school, such as out-dated geography books, no longer in use.

"The work of the bureaucrats," he sighs. "We had to take control."

A long time ago the young people began to ignore the warnings of their elders. They would kill animals needlessly and began to do the same with the fish they caught, maiming them and throwing them back in the lake. Now, in those days, animals, fish and birds were known to have supernatural powers and so the elders lived in constant dread of the catastrophe they knew would happen.

One day it began to rain. Soon all the waters rose and covered the world. Many people perished. Of the survivors, there was an old woman who had an only daughter.

"This is the great catastrophe that we have been expecting," said the old woman to her daughter. "It has been caused by the thoughtlessness of our young people, and as you were always mindful of what I said, I am going to save you while I can. The others shall be destroyed because the waters are continually rising."

One cold, spring morning Rod Robinson, executive director of the Nisga'a Tribal Council, rumbles down the Nass valley in his 4X4 truck, through the lava fields that shape his ancestral lands.

Trailing a plume of lava dust in his wake, Rod is travelling from the tribal centre of Gitlakdamiks, past the foot suspension bridge that swings across the Nass River.

Two hundred and fifty years ago the volcano Wilksi Baxhl Mihl erupted in the lower Nass. Blazing lava instantly covered two villages, killing 2,000 people and shunting the riverbed clear across the valley. The fiery explosion and its towering cloud of ash was seen and heard by white traders as far away as the Pacific coast, who wrote in their logbook that following the eruption a blast of hot air flowed downriver. Today the vast lava fields with their sooty iridescence are sacred ground to the Nisga'a.

The valley is the wealth of the Nisga'a, a storehouse that produced a civilization as rich in art and family history as that of Renaissance Italy long before the European sailing ships arrived on the West Coast in the eighteenth century. This is a culture that transforms everything — masks, spoons, totem poles, the cedar panels of finely-wrought long houses — into elaborate works of art.

Rod pulls up near a bend in the river where the murky brown waters appear to coil back on themselves. In a light drizzle under a rising cloud cover, he watches technician George Gosnell operate a large, rotating fish wheel that scoops salmon from the river. Grappling a silver chinook onto the scale, George expertly weighs, measures and tags his wriggling catch, all in less than sixty seconds. Then, carefully cupping the magnificent fish in his hands, he bends to release it back into the fast-running current. Motionless for a second, the chinook rights itself with wavering fins, then darts upriver in a series of quick, bright angles.

The first run of chinook salmon are known as hangwooyim, they are smaller. Then come the very large chinook salmon known as anhamook. Then come the sockeye in large numbers. Then pinks, or humpbacks, then dog salmon. Last come the coho. The coho still run in October. If there are lots of fish, we get coho after the New Year.

A stately figure whose silver hair testifies to many years of "the struggle" to settle his nation's land claim, Rod emotes the implacable patience and pragmatism that helps to explain Nisga'a resolve: "We will never give up our rightful struggle to control our territory and govern ourselves."

Rod has spent much of his adult life wrangling with interchangeable teams of government negotiators, fighting within the framework of Canada's justice system, to settle a claim that has dragged on — past contempt, past anger — into a cruel and unending charade. A charade cloaked in denial by a country unwilling to admit the racism rooted in its founding institutions.

Meanwhile, there is unrelenting pressure from multinational corporations for Nisga'a resources, especially the forests. The scorched earth of clearcuts, the salmon streams that have been mauled by bulldozers and choked to death by logging debris offer dramatic proof that here in the Nass, as everywhere else in the world, human shortsightedness and greed almost always lead to overexploitation.

"We were appalled by the cut-and-run logging," Rod says, guiding his truck around a large pothole on the gravel surface. "It's very depressing. That's why we've been very vocal about it.

"One time they blew up the beaver dams. The dams were flooding the main road here, and the company had to have the road to get the timber out.

"They blew up the dams," Rod says, still incredulous. "They hired somebody to trap the beaver first, then dynamited the dams. There were salmon and oolichan carcasses all around."

This heedless action stands in stark contrast to the Nisga'a concept of the "Common Bowl" that predates by millennia the notion of sustainable development that has become a latter-day mantra for environmentalists.

We eat the roots of one type of plant, the leaves of another. We make medicine from the roots of trees. We eat what comes from the hemlock, spruce, jack pine and balsam, for medicine. All the trees and different leaves in the Nass we use—this is what the white man has taken out. They think the trees are for nothing. The trees are there for a purpose. They are just like us. We're all born for a purpose, for a job in this world. Some of us do lots, some of us a little. But we're all used for one thing or another.

"It's greed, plain and simple, that ravages our fish stocks and rips the gold and silver from our mountains. It's greed that keeps 30,000 truckloads of logs worth $60 million a year grinding out of the Nass.

"And what do we get?" asks Rod. "Not a penny."

Unrestrained logging and inadequate reforestation have also dimmed job prospects in the forest industry for the Nisga'a, with unemployment climbing to eighty per cent, quadruple the rate a few years ago. An independent study found in the early 1980s that 36,000 hectares had not been adequately reforested. In the upper Nass, clearcuts are as large as 6,000 hectares. "Look at our river. Look at our creeks," he says. "All damaged."

Back in his office at Gitlakdamiks, Rod welcomes a visitor who has come to the tribal territory in an attempt to understand the Land Question; what the Nisga'a hope to achieve in their long struggle to have aboriginal title recognized by the governments of Canada and British Columbia.

Rod had his own struggles.

He is one of the Nisga'a who as a young man left the community to work "outside." Like many of his generation, he was sent at the age of eight to residential school at Alert Bay, a long and lonely trip over the roiling waters of Hecate Strait.

At seventeen, Rod attended high school in Prince Rupert, a city that was closer to home and friendlier, as many Nisga'a lived and worked in the canneries and other labouring jobs. Rod unloaded fish at Sunnyside Cannery—a dirty job, he recalls—after school, then graded fish at a cold-storage plant.

In those days traditional Nisga'a culture—so strong in the memory of the elders—was derided by non-natives as a nuisance interfering with commerce. "They looked down on us," he recalls.

Rod became a fish-grader foreman, but after five years bought a gillnetter, and later worked on a seine boat. But as fishing was (and still is) a seasonal occupation, he went ashore for good when he saw a poster advertising jobs for loggers.

He made big money in the woods, working his way up from chokerman to faller, from boom foreman to river-drive foreman, from cat and skidder driver to loader operator and again to foreman. Along the way, he married, and raised a family of ten children.

But increasingly incensed at the cut-and-run logging in the Nass, Rod decided to move back home. In 1952 he took his place in the deliberations of the four clans that make up Nisga'a society, helping the council develop a land policy.

Folding his hands, Rod settles in behind his desk in the modest wood-panelled office he shares with other tribal council officials. Beside the phone and a stack of messages sit two well-thumbed paperbacks—one on stress, the other on Christianity.

A lay reader in the Anglican Church, Rod sees no contradiction between ancient Nisga'a beliefs and contemporary Christianity. On the contrary, he points to parallels between the Bible and Ayuukhl Nisga'a and draws spiritual strength from both. It is the teachings of Ayuukhl Nisga'a though, that define his Nisga'a name, his crest and his clan.

"I must serve as a role model," explains the man who has devoted thirty years of his life to the struggle. It is this self-sacrifice that lies at the heart of the devotion he inspires, giving dignity and hope to every one of his people who see for themselves what commitment can accomplish.

"The code instructs us not to use strong language, not to insult those who oppose us," Rod says. "We are taught to respect everyone's way of life. Share our land, yes. But never give it away."

In war, we never backed down from anything. If one of our warriors was killed we did not run away. We put up a fight to show we had the authority to whatever belonged to us. Otherwise, we would be wiped out. God gave us this land, and we were always victorious in our encounters with other tribes.

Chief Txaalaxhatkw and daughter singing into ethnologist Marius Barbeau's phonograph

By 1993, the Nisga'a had been in formal land claims negotiations with the federal government for almost twenty years, since a split decision by the Supreme Court of Canada opened up the question of aboriginal title. Victoria agreed to join negotiations in 1991, reversing its historical stand that aboriginal title was a dead issue.

An agreement-in-principle, an important step towards a final agreement in which major issues of jurisdiction and land title would be settled, was to have been signed by March 1993. But that deadline—like so many others—came and went.

Still, the Nisga'a press on. Ever planning for the future, they are now fine-tuning a blueprint for self-government.

"As we have said many times, we don't want to secede as a separate state or sell the land, but we do want to control its use," says Rod Robinson. "We will work with the governments and the resource industries, yes, but we will make the important decisions.

"We will collect taxes, too—possibly through an agreement to return federal and provincial levies—and use the revenue to help administer our lands, instead of existing on federal funding as we now do."

The four Nisga'a villages would tax their residents to pay for utilities and services, as other municipalities do. "There might be some grumbling, even in our villages," he concedes. "It's hard for people to accept change. But they will, after a while, if it benefits them."

Rod tells of the disappointment he, Hubert Doolan, Frank Calder, and the late James Gosnell felt when the Supreme Court of Canada failed to agree on a clear verdict on aboriginal title in 1973. It was James Gosnell who shook many Canadians from their complacency on native issues when he declared the Nisga'a own their ancestral lands "lock, stock and barrel." And it was Frank Calder who, on behalf of the Nisga'a, sued the provincial government for title.

"Why are you hanging your heads, the elders asked us," Rod says, recalling the technical loss in Supreme Court. "The highest court in the land cannot erase you. The land will still be here. The river has run since time immemorial."

This fierce certainty will persist until an agreement is finally reached. "The governments are dragging their feet," Rod says. "They are confused. And cannot realize the advantages—for all Canadians—of a self-sustaining aboriginal economy."

The Nisga'a first met European traders in the latter part of the eighteenth century, scorning British explorer Captain George Vancouver because he had nothing of value to trade for seal fur.

The traders were followed by the missionaries, who, with Christian zeal, persuaded the Nisga'a to chop down the totem poles the missionaries feared as symbols of idolatry. Working with the government, they began the "civilizing" process that wrenched children from their homes and sent them off to learn the white man's culture in residential schools.

It was generations before the churchmen began to understand that they were destroying a vital, dynamic culture so different from their own. Today the Christian churches support the Nisga'a and many Nisga'a leaders consider the church one of their strongest allies and supporters.

Later, settlers began making their way up Portland Canal to the mouth of the Nass, claiming Nisga'a land. The British Columbia colonial government had refused to recognize aboriginal rights before and after it joined in the confederation of Canada in 1871, and a desultory dialogue began between Victoria and Ottawa.

The federal government first insisted the province abide by the Royal Proclamation of 1763 which decreed that treaties must be made with native peoples to take over their land. But Victoria gave way under the pressure of settlers and developers, and refused to recognize title, much less to negotiate.

In 1884 the federal government outlawed the potlatch—the gift-giving feast that anchored tribal society. The feast was, in essence, the seat of government for the Nisga'a and other west coast tribes. From 1884 to 1951, attendance at a potlatch was punishable by jail terms of two to six months.

By 1920, the Indian Act was amended to require the compulsory attendance of Indian children in schools. The express purpose of the schools was to teach children that their parents' ways of life were "savage" and that "civilization"—meaning white society—was their only hope. In 1920 the Indian department's deputy superintendent, Duncan Campbell Scott, made it all too clear: "Our object is to continue until there is not a single Indian in Canada that has not been absorbed into the body politic, and there is no Indian question and no Indian department."

This is the white man's world. It's not our world anymore. But it's still our land—our culture is still there. If we are going to survive we have to send our children to school, whether we like it or not. I have said that our land guarantees our education in the white man's world forever. The white man cannot pay for our land—it is priceless. It guarantees our medical needs and taxation, our contribution to the country. It guarantees everything. That is why we say Nisga'a land is not for sale. We cannot sell it. Because without the land, what is going to be our survival?

Until 1948, Indians were expressly denied municipal voting rights. In 1949 they were finally awarded provincial voting rights. It was not until 1961 that they gained a vote—and a voice—in federal elections.

All the while the Nisga'a continued their protest. To settle the Land Question, Sim'oogit Sganisim Sim'oogit led the first land claims delegation to Victoria in 1881. It was turned aside rudely. A later delegation to Ottawa returned to the Nass with some vague assurances, and Nisga'a Chief Israel Sgat'iin banished the surveyors the provincial government had sent to stake out reserves to pen the Nisga'a in isolated fragments of their ancestral land.

"'What's that in your canoe?' the chief asked, pointing to a transit and other survey equipment," Rod Robinson relates the history.

"The surveyors told him they were going to give us land, and the chief asked how he could give us land that was already ours. 'These are our mountains and our river,' Chief Sgat'iin said. Then he pointed his blunderbuss in the head surveyor's belly, took away the surveying instruments and sent him back downstream.

"Of course, the white surveyors came back. Eventually our reserves were laid out as sixty plots—the size of postage stamps—making up less than one per cent of our traditional territory.

"We countered one rebuff after another," Rod continues. "In 1913 we appealed to the highest court in the land by sending a petition to the Privy Council of England. The document, which spelled out our claim to our land, became a rallying cry for other tribes."

In 1916 after sporadic attempts at dialogue, the Nisga'a joined with The Allied Tribes of British Columbia to force government recognition. Then the government cracked down, prohibiting Indian fund raising that effectively quashed all land claims discussion. It was 1951 before the government backed down and repealed this repressive legislation.

Formed in 1955, the Nisga'a Tribal Council united the four Nisga'a clans and their four communities to work towards resolving their land claim.

Nisga'a chief Frank Calder, the first Indian to be elected to a legislature in the British Commonwealth when he became a Member of the Legislative Assembly of British Columbia in 1949, spearheaded this historic initiative. Elected as the first president of the council, Calder led the Nisga'a into the next stage of their political evolution. Through its efforts, the council was instrumental in affecting a fundamental shift in federal government policy towards aboriginal peoples.

"In 1964 we decided to sue the provincial government for aboriginal title," says Rod. "The case wound up in the Supreme Court of Canada and set the stage for the negotiations that are still going on."

And while the Nisga'a struggle simmers, the increasingly fractious fight for aboriginal rights—in Canada and around the world—has heated past the boiling point.

A bloody confrontation between Mohawk Indians and Quebec police at Oka in 1990 vaulted Canada's treatment of its aboriginal peoples onto the world stage and embarrassed the Canadian government.

Unresolved land claims have also become an economic minefield for Canadian businesses loath to invest in projects on contested land.

Meanwhile, a growing respect for aboriginal culture has crossed over into popular thinking. Driven by the increasingly common view that something is terribly awry with modern life, many people appear to suffer from a crisis of identity in an incoherent world.

"There is a sense that economic growth and prosperity are not enough any more," says Rod. "Being part of a community, being really connected to each another in your own place are what really count. That is what our ancient stories tell us. We are willing to share those stories with white people. If only they would listen."

Women are the strength of the Nisga'a. "A generation of our men—those working on the Land Question—has been forced to live out of suitcases and hotel rooms. We raise their children, help them cope, help them look good."

Cheryl Doolan is a compact, revving engine of a woman with trim brown hair and glasses. One blustery morning in late April, she leans over the railing of the ferry sailing north from Prince Rupert, into the wind-whipped waters of Portland Canal, and on to her home in the tiny fishing village of Gingolx. After attending the Nisga'a annual convention in Terrace, Cheryl is in an expansive mood. After four days of careful listening, she welcomes a chance to talk.

Situated at the mouth of the Nass River, perched on the westernmost tip of Nisga'a territory where the Alaska Panhandle intersects the British Columbia coast, Gingolx is isolated by its geography. With no road to link it to upriver Nisga'a communities, the village of 400 can be reached only by float plane, fishing boat or five-hour ferry trip that sails, weather permitting, twice weekly from Prince Rupert.

Cheryl is a true believer. She wants—she demands—self-government for her people and has applied her considerable talents and non-stop energy to bring it about. But beyond the rhetoric and legal wrangling, Cheryl sees self-government in very human terms.

"Self-government means individual responsibility, respect for your neighbour's rights and unity of purpose," she says. "This is easier said than done for a people who have lived their lives in poverty, whose every aspect of their lives was controlled by the Department of Indian Affairs."

The ferry swings northeast. In late spring, the deep waters of the inlet, whipped by winds plunging down the steep basalt rock of the Coast Mountains, can turn a stomach. These are the same waters where generations of Nisga'a fished for salmon, halibut and a bounty of other marine life. Onshore, looming out of the blue-green landscape, are the tumble-down remains of a cannery, one of many, where earlier this century many Nisga'a men and women loaded and filleted fish for white owners.

Cheryl tells the story of how, as a girl of fourteen, she left her parents—"a devastating experience"—to attend high school in North Vancouver, boarding at the home of the Rundgrens, a white family. She studied hard and made good marks.

After finishing her Grade 12, she did not attend graduation ceremonies "because my parents could not afford to buy me a dress or fly south for the ceremony."

Teary-eyed, Cheryl waved good-bye to her classmates who sent her off with a bouquet of roses. She headed home, diploma in hand, to settle back into village life. She married husband Stuart and raised three children—Rachel, Fraser and Karla. Later, she began to work with the local band council and, over time, took on-the-job training to become the village's only social worker. Today, besides managing a full-time caseload, Cheryl is active in tribal life including women's church groups, choir, youth groups and girls' majorettes.

"I'm on so many committees," she says, "I can't remember them all. I get home from work and rush back out the door for another meeting. But I just can't relax when there is so much to be done. Ever since I was eight years old, my dream has been to work for my people."

In 1969, Cheryl and Stuart moved to Prince Rupert, the harbour town that served as base for his fishpacking operation. The meaner streets of Rupert provided a cautionary tale for Cheryl who was struck by

Facing page: Gwilks'anooksim hanak', Proud Woman mask

the stress of city life. "There is so much family violence in cities. There's no time for children to be just children. We had to be on guard, to watch out for our kids all the time."

By contrast, as a child Cheryl worked happily at her mother's side, learning to string oolichan, fillet sea lion and pick the ripest soapberries to preserve. Now her children have grown and Cheryl is teaching these skills to granddaughter Sinobo, whom she is helping to raise. In the matrilineal culture of the Nisga'a, parents do not handle the discipline or the problems of the children. Parents nurture and love. Uncles and aunts, a bit more distant from the youngsters, mete out discipline and solve problems.

From her mother Rose, Cheryl learned the elaborate food preparation integral to Nisga'a feasts, for which planning often begins a year in advance. She is proud of the culinary tradition that has earned her village its far-flung reputation.

"Gingolx is known for its golden hospitality," she says. "We show our visitors warmth, friendliness and great food. Crab and halibut are specialties, simply the best. "

When people had done enough harvesting of salmon they would fill up their boxes with bundles of fish — enough for themselves and, on top of that, they made allowances for visitors who never left the chief's house empty-handed, because he was always prepared. We did not expect any payment for having people stay at our homes. We just made sure there would be enough dried fish. There would also be berries, soapberries. When we returned, our father's canoe would be loaded.

"I was blessed," Cheryl says. "My family taught me dignity and pride. As a mother, I always put my family first. And it doesn't stop when the children grow up. Even today, my daughters bring pot-luck dinners to my house. It's the Nisga'a way. We don't eat alone."

Gingolx harbour. The captain cuts the engine and the ferry glides silently through a wispy, grey mist. The sudden quiet adds an empyrean quality to a landscape of fishing boats and scattered wooden houses, dominated by the tall white spire of the Anglican church.

The ferry bounces off the wooden pilings of the government wharf, shuddering to a halt. Hefting her bags, eager to disembark, eager to get home, Cheryl strides down the deck, pauses, then calls out over her shoulder: "When we settle the Land Question — and I know we will — we just might get our lives back again. I pray it happens soon."

The Nisga'a story goes back beyond recorded history—to a flood, when the glaciers of the Ice Age were melting. Tribal legends tell of ancestors surviving on rafts lashed to the mountain tops. To a time when Txeemsim (Clem-sum)—trickster, miracle worker and pivotal figure of Nisga'a cosmology—came down from his sky home to do the bidding of K'amligihahlhaahl or Chief of Heavens.

When Txeemsim appeared on earth, our ancestors lived in twilight, disorder and the constant threat of starvation. Txeemsim's life was one of constant struggle with hunger and survival. He had to learn the necessary self-discipline and knowledge. Even Txeemsim, with all his supernatural powers, had to learn to survive and share with others.

Txeemsim was a supernatural being, Bert McKay explains to his class, who assumed human and animal forms when the world was still in twilight. Like the Greek god Prometheus, he stole the fire of heaven and brought it back to earth; back to a people huddled in a forbidding, frozen landscape.

Like those of Sophocles and Aeschylus, Txeemsim's moral dilemmas recall a time when human society, organized in small tribal groups, fought for its very survival. Like the gods of Greek mythology, the Naxnok or spirit beings of the ancient Nisga'a world were manifestations of human hopes and fears.

Bert tells the class that Txeemsim plays the role of "transformer" similar to the coyote trickster of the Navaho and the raven of Haida myth. Indeed, Txeemsim is sometimes called "raven".

"Txeemsim displays the best of what humankind should strive for," says Bert. "But he's an approachable demi-god, full of human failings, even as he demonstrates how these failings can be conquered.

Over time, our ancestors learned that it was in their own best interests to accept moral responsibility.

"And although Txeemsim was kindly and possessed a keen sense of humour, he was also thief, trickster and liar. Obscenely greedy with an insatiable curiosity, he sometimes made trouble for trouble's sake.

"To ensure his hard-won lessons weren't wasted, this trickster wandered up and down the river, teaching the people he met. This was how our system of oral history began."

Txeemsim created many Nass landscapes. "Between Iceberg Bay and Nasoga Gulf he made a large mountain," Bert continues. "After bringing the oolichan to the Nass River, he wished to protect our fishing grounds from the Haida and Tsimshian. So he hurled a mountain into the channel. Txeemsim also magically flattened the valley between the four mountains so we could build our long houses. He moulded the channels of the Nass River so that more salmon would spawn and taught us the sacred value of place.

"The deeds and misdeeds of Txeemsim show that every creature in the universe and every person in society has a rightful and meaningful role to play; that we need each other. Because of this mutual need, Txeemsim proved that every single action or decision we make is actually a moral one. It will affect others, for good or bad. Over and over, Txeemsim's life proves that selfish behaviour is ultimately destructive for both self and society," Bert says.

The bell rings. School is out. Bert stands to make his final point. "I tell you about Txeemsim," he explains to another generation of Nisga'a leaders, "because he is the touchstone of our identity, our history. Txeemsim and Nisga'a are one in the same."

After a Settlement Feast at Gitwinksihlkw, Nelson Leeson drives home slowly through the lava fields. It is past midnight and his passenger, a visitor from Vancouver, will stay the night at the Leeson home. The visitor keeps asking questions about Nisga'a culture and customs as they drive the switchbacks of the braided valley, through the spruce forest and all the way to the bridge that crosses the Nass River east of Lakalzap. In the middle of the concrete span, Nelson shuts off the motor and rolls the vehicle to a stop. He climbs out and walks down the bridge and into the night. It is silent except for the river churning below. Jagged stars flare across the northern sky. Suddenly, Nelson re-appears in the headlights. He flings his long arms into the night air. "We're all human beings," he shouts. "We all need a place to live. The Nass is our place."

Chief Ksim Xsaan's throne

Beyond the clouds surrounding the highest peak at Magoonhl Lisims, the headwaters of Nass River, somewhere "above", is the home of our Chief in Heavens, our Creator. This we learned from our ancestors, who in turn learned it from His messengers, and in particular, from His grandson, Txeemsim.

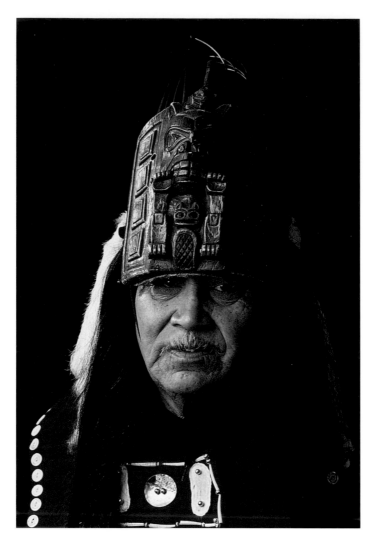

Gordon McKay, Eagle clan

What we don't like about the government is their saying this: "We will give you this much land." How can they give it when it is our own? We cannot understand it. They have never bought it from us or our forefathers. They have never fought and conquered our people and taken the land in that way, and yet they say now that they will give us so much land—our own land.

The ancient people, our ancestors, were given animals to be used as crests by each wilp. The crest animals are the ones which showed them how to live, what to eat, and how to catch and prepare the different food animals. This is how our forefathers lived.

Facing page: Ancient petroglyphs on a rock outcrop in the middle of the Nass River

The people didn't just live anywhere they pleased. No, you lived by your own water. People cut out their land wherever there was fish — that is where our forefathers lived. They lived on the edge of that water. The reason why we lived on this river is because of the source of transportation. The transportation was the canoe, in those days. The source of livelihood was the salmon.

That is why we lived there.

Nass River below Lakalzap

Salome McKay, Wolf clan

We all come from the same original mother. The Sigidimnak makes the ultimate decisions regarding names and inheritance. The only limit on a woman's power is at her husband's death, when the personal property goes to his side. When children are born their family ties are with the mother. So, if a woman was an Eagle, her child was an Eagle. The same for the Wolf clan, the Raven clan and the Killer Whale.

Once a great flood covered the world. When the rains stopped the Nisga'a came out of their sealed logs high on the mountain peaks. This small group of survivors saw that the whole of the Nass Valley was covered in water and thousands of rainbows filled the sky. High above flocks of birds circled with no place to nest. The birds dropped their plumage until the water was covered with feathers. Then the waters began to recede and the world slowly returned to normal.

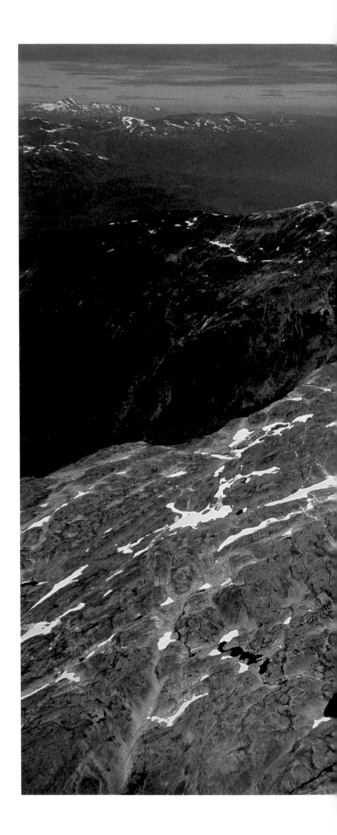

Sgan̓isim X̱hlaawit (Vetter Peak) in central Nass valley

Sgaǹisim Xk'aat'aapgwit (Mt. Kwinamass) south of Gingolx

Sgaǹisim Guxw Mak'iskw (Mt. Fowler) at top of Hastings Arm

Sgaǹisim Laxsẁa (Mt. Hinkley) near tip of Portland Canal

When our Chief of Heavens sent people down to earth they were grouped in four clans. The Eagle clan was one of them, then there was the Wolf clan, the Raven clan and the Killer Whale. These were the specified clans. The crests used were for identification of each family and were recognized as such. Our Chief of Heavens gave our people these crests when they were placed on Lisims, the Nass River. Now he, the Chief of Heavens, gathered together throngs of people and placed them in various locations other than the Nass River. They were informed that they will not speak the same dialect. There would be a distinct difference according to where these people are placed. There shall be one tongue spoken on the Nass River, from the headwaters right down to the estuary. Fluent speaking and understanding would be prevalent among them, but not so with the others. 'The other dialects you will not clearly understand' is what the Chief of Heavens said when he placed them here on earth. Their destination was unknown and uncertain. Our forefathers (the Wahlingigat) did not bring anything with them. It was dark on earth then. There were bodies of land, but barely visible. There was no light or water then. The land was like mountains where they were. Our ancestors made preparations to make it their homeland. The first location on Lisims for their new community was at Gwinsk'eexkw, 'village in darkness'. These people were the first occupants of the Valley, and this was their first village. Soon buildings were erected. There were four different Houses. The people intermarried with other families placed here with them. Four females were with the other representatives of the clans. One woman was Ksim Laxsgiik. Another was Ksim Laxgibuu. Another was Ksim Ganada. The other was Ksim Neekhl (or Ksim Gisk'ahaast). When children were born their family ties were with their mother. So that, if a woman was an Eagle, the child naturally was an Eagle. The same applied to the Wolf clan, the Raven clan and the Killer Whale. They erected their village at Lax Gwinsk'eexkw, on an island near Gitlaxt'aamiks, on Lisims. Bark was utilized for house walls, also for roofing. There were trees above the village, and these were used whole ... for stringers and roof ridges. Upon completion each House started raising families. The village population began to increase.

Rod Robinson, Eagle clan

Timber Wolf

K'amluugidis had been out hunting for his family when he was
approached by a wounded wolf. This wolf had a big deer bone lodged in
the back of its throat. K'amluugidis walked right up to this animal and
he removed the bone from its throat. K'amluugidis saved this wolf's life.
The wolf was very grateful, and he told the chief, "I will call you ...
when you hear me calling K'amluugidis ... you come up to me and I
will give you food." Soon after, K'amluugidis did hear the wolves call his
name. He walked in the direction of where the wolves had called and
K'amluugidis found a deer carcass. This was very timely as the people
were about to die of starvation. It was then that K'amluugidis returned
his thanks to these animals by adopting the wolf as a crest.

Jacob Nyce, Wolf clan

Totem pole at Gitwinksihlkw

Facing page: Chester Moore, Raven clan

Killer Whales

Then suddenly the leader of the killer whales jumped high into the air and then dove back into the sea and was seen no more. While the rest of the killer whales continued to jump and dive around them, the father and his younger son stood at shore, their eyes filled with tears, their hearts filled with sorrow, as they mourned the loss of the man they had both deeply loved. And as they stood there crying, a tall, strong man emerged from the water. He was the older brother who had returned to live with them once more. That is when the Killer Whale crest was adopted among the Nisga'a.

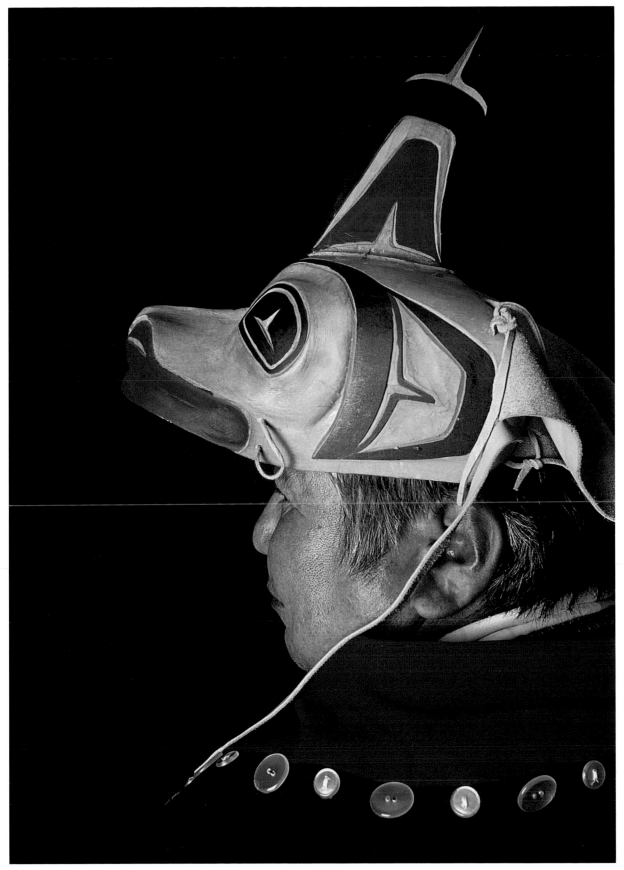

Edward Azak, Killer Whale clan

Galsgiyst, in Observatory Inlet, looking south

The river flowing in the Nass Valley — that belongs to us. All the rocks belong to us; all of the silt in our waters belongs to us. The sand, that belongs to us. All the mineral resources, the mountains, belong to us. The land, the trees, belong to us.

T'aam Anlibaykw (Amoth Lake)

The waters always come from the mountains. That is the reason the mountains are named so it will be known what place the water comes from, [and] who owns it.

Spoons carved from Mountain Goat horn

That is when I saw how they dried Mountain Goat, which was really tasty. My mother would skin the goat and showed me how to make the wool out of the hide. Each time it rolls out of my hand I'd get so mad; it was all done by hand, not machine. They used this wool to make slippers, gloves and socks. My mother dried the goat meat and we ate it. She'd also soften [a] small goat hide and made a ceremonial drum out of it. They also made shoes and men's pants out of it.

Facing Page: Mountain Goats

Before leaving to pursue the wily matx (mountain goat) on the steep slopes of the Xts'imat'iin, X'anmas and Lax Kswan mountain peaks, Wiigat knew now from experience and the teachings of his heavenly grandfather, that he must prepare properly for the hunt. Out of respect for the souls of the animals he plans to hunt, he must fast and cleanse himself beforehand. During the last four days prior to his departure, Wiigat bathed in the spring and with a mouthful of spring water made a 'Box' (wish) that the mountain goats would let him be successful in the hunt. "I got hit, slapped on the hands, [while in the mountains on a mountain goat hunt] when I tried to eat the blue berries ... they looked so tempting and delicious. For it's against the rules to eat before the kill."

Facing Page: Dancer Dennis Nyce representing Naxnok, or spirit beings

Vetter Falls in Lava Bed Memorial Park

Each little place has a name. Every so far in distances there is a name for [the] resting place; or where two properties meet; or this is where they turn around at the end of each day. So they know how far they had gone.

A medicinal blend of cedar tree fronds, Kaak'hise (the leaves of a small plant which grows in mountain crevices), spruce pitch and salmon roe was used to heal and prevent infection of a major wound or a very bad cut. The salmon roe made the blend soft so it would not congeal. The mixture was spread on a leaf and applied to the wound directly.

Shikss or Highbush cranberries

Oscar Swanson's oolichan crew at Fishery Bay

And those that were kind hearted called the young men together to go along with them to get oolichan for everybody. The Nisga'a ways were to help one another in everything they do.

Henry McKay

Two young Nisga'a from Lakalzap carrying an oolichan box

When the snow started to melt the Wahlingigat knew that the first species of fish was about to hit the river. These fish were 'saak', or oolichans, which arrived in great numbers. All types of sea life followed this species wherever they went. There were many predators of this fish and, when it was realized that these sea mammals were roaming the estuary in large hordes, then our people started dipping their nets. The method of dipping for saak used the larger of the two types of dip-nets, the hlist. In those very early times, a favorite spot for dip-netting oolichans was at Ts'im Anwiihlist, located just above the present day Grease Harbor. This was how far upriver the oolichan run went in those days.

Clarence Stevens, Larry Martin and Albert Stephens cooking oolichan to extract oil in vats at Fishery Bay

The grease was squeezed out of the oolichan before it was cooked by pressing the oolichan between boards. The squeezed oolichan were then placed in the wooden boxes and water and red hot rocks introduced. In the old days ... they made strainers to squeeze out the grease in the oolichan before they cooked it. They put heavy rocks on these big boards to squeeze out the grease. The inside of the gal'ink was real thick where they put these hot rocks. They put water in to boil the oolichans. They didn't have clocks in those days.

Lakalzap, Nass River

After smoked and sun-dried oolichan were properly dried they would be taken down and stored. After that is done it is time to get wild rice. Also the time to get the delicacy called ksuuw. Ksuuw was also considered a medicine. I think that's why no one had trouble with appendicitis in the old days. {It was} also the time to get a new supply of cedar strips for making rope, baskets, and stringing oolichan.

Sun-drying oolichan outside smokehouse

Wilma Moore and granddaughter Gabrielle stringing oolichan on cedar strips

We have one bowl to eat from in this valley, the bowl is known as Ts'ak'hl Nisga'a, Nisga'a Bowl.

There is only one river where the Nisga'a sat on the banks, known and called Lisims.

Facing Page: Stringing oolichan with cedar strips

You respect the creatures, the fish, the fowl of the air, and the animals. We don't allow our fish to rot without using it, you know, it is forbidden. You take what you need and what you need to survive — only — and leave the rest, that's conservation . . . You know exactly what you need for the winter, how many of you [are] in there. How much dried salmon you have to have, how much oolichan grease, this sort of thing. You can process more oolichan grease than you need, then go out to the people that live by the sea and trade for some seaweed and herring eggs . . . abalone, clams and cockles.

Halibut being smoked

Vince Stevens

Nancy Stephens of Lakalzap preparing salmon for smoking

They all had smokehouses and there was so much fish and the smokehouses were full all the time. When the fish were ready and dried, they would be replaced. We did everything, made rotten fish eggs known as caviar. There's forty fish to a bundle. We use all parts of the fish, salted fish. We got everything. That was also dried and salted, there was no bottles in those days. We picked 'milks' (wild crabapples). My mother steamed that. During our free time in the evenings, my mother-in-law mixes water and grease, known as 'hlai-ax', and we mixed these milks with it. We also picked 'sbikss' (Highbush cranberries), and this was mixed the same way as milks. We filled cans, pots, anything with these berries.

Ella Stevens and her mother Lilly with Nikita Stevens (foreground) readying salmon for smokehouse

People often refer to us as rich people, because we can make food of all
kinds in every season. Our land is very rich.

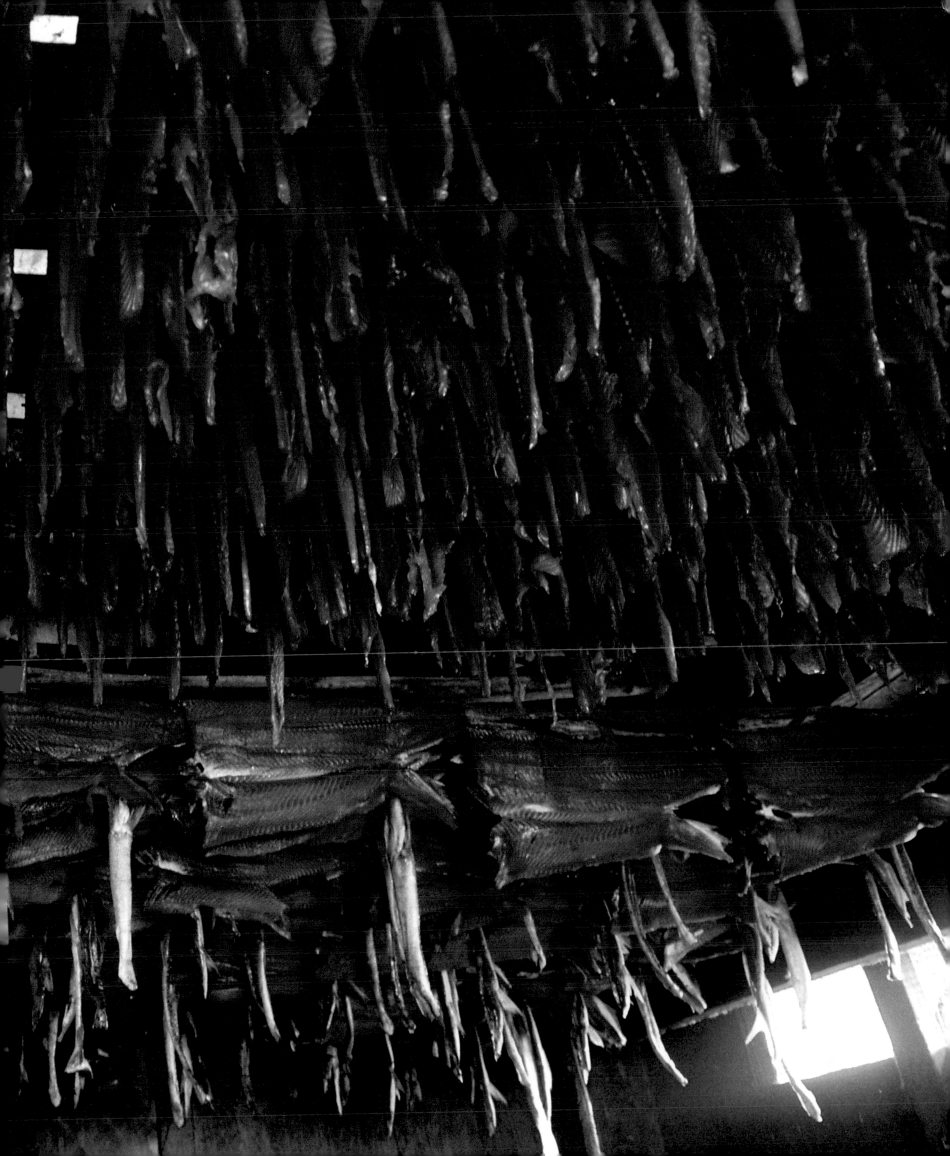

Gingolx, at the mouth of the Nass River

When we first catch the spring salmon or any type of new food we make use of almost all of it. The spring salmon is first cut open, then the insides are taken out; we eat the heart, stomach, liver and eggs. We also eat the head. It is a traditional ritual, when new food is taken after the winter.

Previous Page: Interior of smokehouse

Steven Doolan Jr. at Gingolx dock

Randy Adams with sons Darryl and Clint, mending net at Gingolx

We use the net. The net is woven from 'sdatx' (stinging nettle). The net is not new to us, we had the net before the white man came. We use a big mesh for spring salmon, small mesh for sockeye. You have to go real early in the morning. And you don't set just anywhere in the river.

Craig Doolan with sockeye salmon caught on his grandfather's gillnetter in Nass Bay

Treaty Creek, traditional boundary line between Nisga'a and Tahltan

Sdox Yansgwit, on Ishkheenickh River, where legend says Txeemsim placed a large mountain from the coast

And the ango'oskw is mapped out in such a way they have a name here, a
name there, and that's the boundary of the ango'oskw.

Before the volcanic explosion the Gitwinksihlkw wilps lived in a village called Lax Ksi Luux. It was a very large village. It was the largest Nass village before the eruption. In the village of Ksi Luux the chiefs were the government. There were four main chiefs in each village. Wii Seeks was the head chief, then Baxk'ap, then Gwiixmaaw, and finally Naaws. Lesser chiefs came behind each of the main chiefs. When the children were playing with the fish in the river, the chiefs warned them not to. It wasn't just recently that this word 'axgoot' (irresponsibility) started up. It was a long time ago that irresponsible people started increasing in number. After the chiefs warned them, they went back and started playing with the fish again. At night they'd tear the bark off the trees; then they'd roll them up, then set fire to them. Then they'd stick them in the backs of the fish. The fish looked like boats with lights swimming in water at night. The chiefs warned them again and again, but they would not listen. The Great Spirit then got angry with them. The chiefs warned the children they were being disrespectful. When the chiefs heard what had been going on they expected something to happen.

They expected the Great Spirit to use either fire (lakw) or water to kill them all.

Previous Page: Lax Syoon (Bear Pass Glacier) near Stewart, site of an ancient territorial battle

Harold Wright, relating volcano story

So they sent men to watch for such a thing. Some men would watch at night and some would watch in the morning. All of a sudden they heard a rumbling noise in the upper part of the valley which sounded like the rumbling of a number of drums. The people did not expect or see the lava rock coming their way. About two thousand people were killed. About two thousand people of Gitwinksihlkw were still alive. At that time they were know as 'Gitlaxksiluux'.

Crater formed when the volcano erupted 250 years ago, killing 2,000 Nisga'a

School bus crossing the lava beds

Previous Page: Lava beds

Verna Williams teaching a Nisga'a language class

I remember these times because my father took me up to Lax Kswan {ango'oskw}, where he raised me up from a small boy. This place was Hlabikskw's ango'oskw. This is where he taught me how to hunt. He said: "You have to learn how to hunt so you don't starve."

Bradley Doolan and Shane Barton of the Nisga'a Elementary Secondary School Band

Shooting hoops at Lakalzap

Priscilla Nisyok

Gitlakdamiks, with the lava beds and the Nass River in the background

Alice Azak and Mercy Moore weaving cedar strips for ceremonial headdresses

Carved berry bowl

Our grandmothers and grandfathers took great pride in their hard work in preserving their foods. When they were all through and got back home to their village, they invited people to eat with them and taste the foods they'd dried and preserved. This is how our grandparents were, they shared and loved one another.

Gitlakdamiks community hall

Theressa Azak preparing regalia for a feast

The brother or [maternal] nephew who is to inherit the chief's name [and consequently title to the ango'oskw] must put up a feast to take the name passed onto him. The feast requires, in the old days, hoarding wealth for about three years. Great wealth was expended by the old people to acquire the chief's name and to hold title to the ango'oskw. In the old days food and furs were distributed at the feast among the chiefs and prominent people. Today the tradition for passing on names and title to the ango'oskw continues, but money and clothing are used rather than food and furs.

It is the law that after the wedding, then the uncle or grandfather of the bride gives a portion of the land for her berry picking, to get meat or anything that's on the land. When they have children you bring them there to get what you're going to eat. This is called 'bringing your own plate to eat from'. [She] brings the children to show the grounds, so they'll know it belongs to the woman. It is given to her after the marriage.

Previous Page: Marlena Gosnell at the wedding of Shawn Harris and Fern Woods

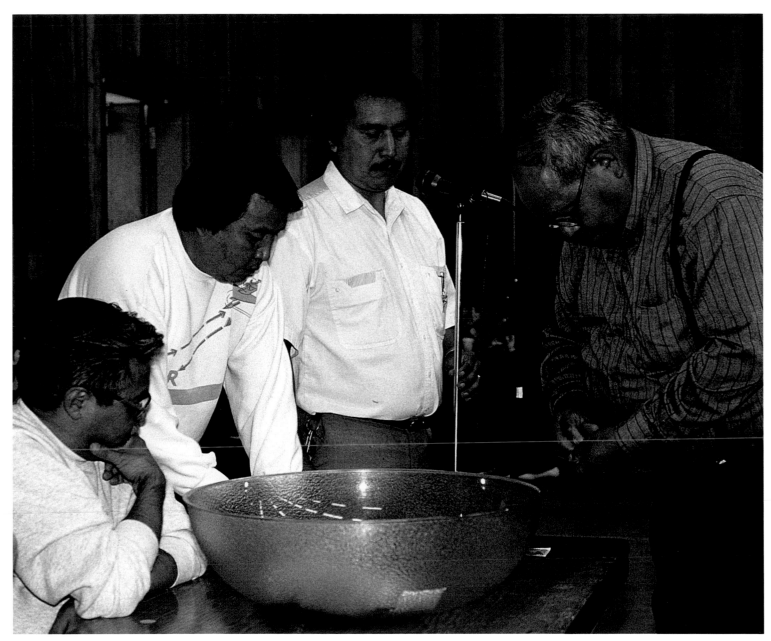

Willard Martin, Perry Azak, Alvin Azak and Charles Swanson at the Settlement Feast, with symbolic "Common Bowl"

Nisga'a dance troop performing at an elders' conference

If the deceased was an important chief, the next chief in the line of his family and tribe who will be taking over his name would invite the people of the whole Nass Valley to a settlement feast called a 'yukw'. It was of vital importance to witness the passing on of a chief's name.

Dancer Raymond Azak at Nisga'a Nation's 36th annual convention

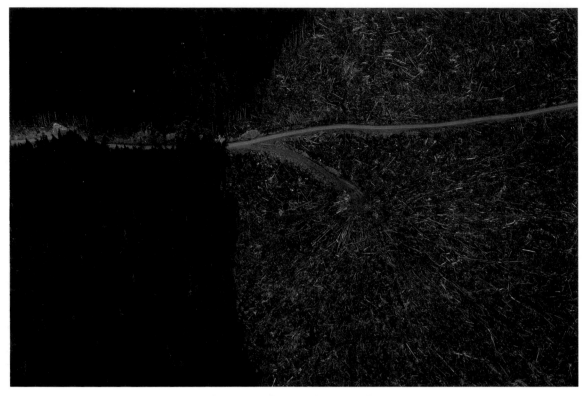

Clearcut in the central Nass Valley

We haven't got any ill feelings in our hearts but we are just waiting for this thing to be settled and we have been waiting for the last five years — it is not only a short time that we have lived here; we have been living here from time immemorial — it has been handed down in legends from the old people and that is what hurts us very much because the white people have come along and taken this land away from us. I myself am an old man and as long as I have lived, my people have been telling me stories about the Flood and they did not tell me that I was only to live here on this land for a short time. We have heard that some white men, it must have been in Ottawa; this white man said that [the Nisga'a] must have been dreaming when they say they own the land upon which they live. It is not a dream — we are certain that this land belongs to us. Right up to this day the government never made any treaty, not even to our grandfathers or our great-grandfathers.

Horace Stevens

Anyox, in Observatory Inlet, site of abandoned copper mine which polluted marine life

You respect the forest and its creatures, the fish, the fowl of the air, and

the animals. We don't allow our fish to rot without using it, you know,

it is forbidden. You take what you need to survive and leave the rest.

That's conservation.

Facing Page: Fertilizing eggs at a salmon enhancement project

Murray Trimble, part of Nisga'a crew loading ships at Somerville Bay

When I spoke at the tribal convention I did not want the white man to destroy anything which is evidence of the truth of our heritage. Those places and that evidence is the basis of our legends, our history. This is the first time I have told you about Wiigat's three fish pits. It is one of our ancestors' landmarks, proof of our history.

Joseph Gosnell Sr., Nisga'a Tribal Council President, outside the Parliament Buildings in Victoria, B.C.

Unity pole outside the school in Gitlakdamiks

Tommy Dennis, Second World War veteran

Gitwinksihlkw on west bank of Nass River is accessible only by foot suspension bridge

Alver Tait, carver, at Gitwinksihlkw

They'd go up this mountain and get a good red cedar. When they find one they'd bring it down to where they'll work on it for a totem pole or just to make planks; the same with yellow cedar. They used it to make canoes with, this red cedar. They build a fire and put big rocks on it. How they fixed the canoes, they chopped them out, the canoe, on the top side. The rocks were getting really hot. They used these thongs they made to pick up the hot rocks. They put the hot rocks all in the canoe they were fixing and the water started boiling. The rocks were this colour [red]. Not long after, then they take the top of the canoes off and take the rocks out. Then the older ones made a boiler out of a birch tree. They never had any planes or jack knives, just a carpenter tool like an axe called T'axwins. These are all made from trees. This was long ago.

Their axe was made of a big stone tied to wood.

Guarding the new pole

Alver Tait performs ceremonial dance to breathe life into the pole before it is raised

The red cedar was the first tree (Simgan) and its use for totem poles, Pts'aan, is especially important to us. On completion of the Pts'aan (totem-pole), the Chief would conduct a ceremony and commemorate the very origin of the Simgan. He sang a Lim'ooy, a song of sorrow or dirge. The Lim'ooy of his forefathers, that was what he sang. After the song the Chief then commemorated the beginning of the Nisga'a ... when the tree was first discovered by them. He remembered all this.

That was the reason for Lim'ooy.

Facing Page: Dorothy Doolan, Alice Azak and Emma Nyce congregate for the pole raising

Nisga'a carry the pole through the streets of Gitwinksihlkw

Randy Adams, Killer Whale clan

When it reached a certain height, the Chief signaled them to stop. The Pts'aan was held at that position while another Chief spoke of other events from the beginning of the Nisga'a. Two Chiefs spoke on the commemoration of events leading to the erecting of the totem pole.

Pole raising in Gitwinksihlkw, the first in 100 years

The people then pulled the totem pole the rest of the way up, lodging the base firmly into the ground. There it stood. Those of you who read this story will come to know and understand it more clearly if you visualize what took place. If you know and your eyes are truly opened to these facts, you will weep, because of its sincerity and truth. You will be moved when you recall what happened thousands of years ago.

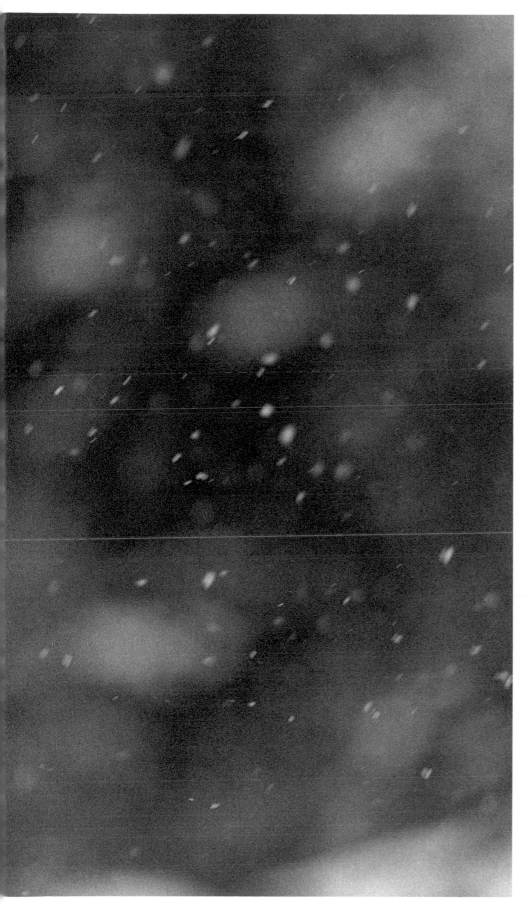

Jacob Nyce, Wolf clan

Cherise Barton, Natasha Venn, Sonobo Doolan at Gingolx

The following is an excerpt of a seminar given by Nisga'a elder Bert McKay at the Vancouver School of Theology in July 1988:

For thousands of years my people have had laws governing land use and ownership. So there was no need for our people to leave our valley and seek other people's lands. Our land was all governed by K'amligihahlhaahl the Supreme God that my people worshipped before the advent of the missionaries. He gave us a place in the world, and when he did this he placed us in the Nass Valley, in a place called Ginsk'eexkw. This is now a historic site—it's in the upper valley—and stories of creation tell us that K'amligihahlhaahl placed four lodges in this place and in each lodge he placed a chieftain and an older sister, a matriarch, and then a wife. And K'amligihahlhaahl identified each of these lodges: you will be known as the Eagle tribe; you will be known as the Wolf tribe; you will be known as the Killer Whale tribe; and you will be known as the Raven tribe. He did this for a reason. He taught our people through his messengers that in order to remain strong and be identified with God's creation we have to hold our family units together.

So that's how the laws began. K'amligihahlhaahl didn't complete the world he gave us. He placed those four lodges, and we say for thousands of years now our people evolved. And, as they matured a new concept was introduced to them, so that after a while there were numerous families, affiliated to those lodges that I have mentioned. And again, K'amligihahlhaahl realized that in order for his people to live in harmony with his creation they must have some guiding principles, they must have a messenger who would show them. So he sent a messenger in the name of Txeemsim and this is how we have evolved today. The Ayuukhl Nisga'a—our code of laws—with the accounts of our history, we have gleaned them from the legends, from the stories, from the examples that Txeemsim gave us. A lot of people who are not versed in our philosophy will hear these stories and probably will scoff at them because they weren't written down as were the legends of other countries. But in every legend Txeemsim presented there was some form of direction included in it and these became the Nisga'a laws. Txeemsim identified ten areas that today we still observe and consider hallowed.

The first is respect. Respect, according to our philosophy, is spelled out this way: when you understand the meaning of respect you have a power that emanates from you and the people around you will respond likewise, they will treat you respectfully. And so, when it comes to the laws of the Nisga'a, if you can't understand the meaning of respect then it means you are going to be running afoul of every area of the Nisga'a law.

Second is education. Our own form of education was already in place and functioning before the first Westerner arrived in our midst. Everyone, according to the Nisga'a law, has some potential to give to the Nisga'a Nation. So there was no classification; everyone was looked upon as a potential member of our society. So, we didn't have words like retardation or misfit or deviant behaviour; no, we are all supposed to be learners, because that's a gift from the creator. Now, in education the people who recommend areas of training are the immediate parents and the grandparents, and here again this was carried out to the last detail. Not all

Ẁii Hoon, Lazarus Moody, boatbuilder

of our people were carvers or master-carvers; not all of them were hunters or fishermen or trappers or trackers or canoe-makers. There were many, many areas within the scope of that education that our people received. But they had to go through a trial-and-error period and it was only then, after going through that, it was realized they could be better fitted for something else. So, in other words, the type of education that was offered was very practical. Number one, all of our people received the edict of preserving life, knowing how to sustain life.

Third was the most important sphere of our laws; that was the law governing the chieftainship and the matriarch. You see, in our culture, the male isn't the dominant figure, rather the female and the male are equally in power. And, more importantly, the matriarch in many ways is far superior to the chieftain for the very simple reason that it is through her that the line of inheritance is passed on.

The fourth and fifth laws deal with the Settlement of the Estate. This happens when a person dies. And it's the only time a name of a chieftain can be transferred to a person. And usually that is done according to the laws laid down by Ayuukhl Nisga'a. In other words, because I'm wealthy (or if I were) I can't just proclaim myself a chief because I have bought that title. No, you have to be reared for it; you have to be disciplined and you have to have the approval of your people before you can take that rank. And today, that's still in place. Under the chieftainship too is our property rights. Again, this was in place before the advent of our western counterparts. There were very strict laws regarding property rights so that there was no need for our people to be going beyond their boundaries to take someone else's property because it was never allowed

Nisga'a brass band in Prince Rupert, 1936

under our laws. I'm a Raven and my father was a Wolf chieftain. According to our law, I was privileged because I was his son, or any of my brothers and sisters were allowed, to harvest from his resource area as long as he was alive. And the minute he died that privilege was given back; I had no claim on his property then. I'm married to a Killer Whale princess and they have resource areas so when we married I was told that because of the children that we were going to have, they will be Killer Whales so I was privileged to feed them from that resource area. As long as my wife lives that will happen. And it's reciprocal. My people would say the same to my wife, but the minute I die that property goes back to us. Our laws, perhaps are edicts, really much more refined because they are constant. They are still observed today.

Preparing Nisga'a stew

according to our laws, a mother has a right to raise children. So under our extended family system this is included. A woman could ask any one of her sisters for whatever child she wants or if that couldn't happen she could ask any one of her cousins. And if that couldn't happen she could go to other members of her clan and usually that went that way. Another way where adoption was used was when there was no successor. For instance, the chieftain, and his sisters, didn't have children, through accident, maybe they were all killed, the chieftain and his sister are allowed to adopt. Now the line, here again, it has to be from the same bloodline if it were possible, especially when this type of inheritance was involved. But if that were not possible then they could go within the clan, within the Raven clan, and select someone who would be the most suitable, the most capable.

Another area that was very important was the institution of marriage. Again, since time immemorial this has been a very sacred institution and we all know why as we do today in the western philosophy; it's through the home that the lifelines are kept, and it's through the home that family values are kept. Since we became Christians it has amplified its true meaning. Under marriage, there are laws which govern adoptions because there are people who cannot have children and

The seventh law governs divorce. Again, this was well in place before our realization that there were western laws. In the Nisga'a tradition, in my own life span, I only know of three cases where divorce has taken place. And that speaks well, because there's over 6,000 Nisga'a today. This was a very strict law. Rather than see a life lost, the marriage was annulled by the ruling chieftain, in consultation with the four ruling chieftains from each of the villages.

Transporting the logs for house construction from Gwinhat'al̓

The eighth law covers war and peace. Through the chieftains this was maintained. In other words, K'amligihahlhaahl gave us enough land, he gave us enough resources so we should be able to use them according to his edicts and we don't have to go outside of our own territory, to take someone else's. And that's the essence of that law.

The ninth law is trading. We were not only just hunters and gatherers, but we were also seafarers; we lived according to the sea. We harvest from the sea as we did on land and from the forests. Trading was very important in our lives.

And the last of our laws, were, I guess you would call them, penalties. One is called restitution, or Ksiiskw. It's a very, very difficult and important law. When a life is lost over carelessness or over greed the law states very plainly, that before the sun sets if the offending family does not settle the issue with the grieved family, then those people have a right to take double the lives that they lost. So the only way that was resolved was by restitution—payment. And then the other part, where certain of the ten laws were broken, not restitution but to make amends, to make a complete break from the shame that you imposed on your family, and that was called public cleansing.

Imbedded in these ten laws is that almighty force we call compassion. That's one of the gifts that each Nisga'a still carries—compassion.

Victorian-style house built by Nisga'a

Facing page: Nisga'a fishermen, Prince Rupert Cannery

PETITION

IN THE MATTER OF THE TERRITORY OF THE NISHGA NATION OR TRIBE OF INDIANS

TO THE KING'S MOST EXCELLENT MAJESTY IN COUNCIL
THE HUMBLE PETITION OF THE NISHGA NATION OR TRIBE OF INDIANS*

SHEWETH AS FOLLOWS:

From time immemorial the said Nation or Tribe of Indians exclusively possessed, occupied and used and exercised sovereignty over that portion of the territory now forming the Province of British Columbia which is included within the following limits, that is to say: – Commencing at a stone situate on the south shore of Kinnamox or Quinamass Bay and marking the boundary line between the territory of the said Nishga Nation or Tribe and that of the Tsimpshean Nation or Tribe of Indians, running thence easterly along said boundary line to the height of land lying between the Naas River and the Skeena River, thence in a line following the height of land surrounding the valley of the Naas River and its tributaries to and including the height of land surrounding the north-west end of Mitseah or Meziadan Lake, thence in a straight line to the northerly end of Portland Canal, thence southerly along the international boundary to the centre line of the passage between Pearse Island and Wales Island, thence south-easterly along said centre line to the centre line of Portland Inlet, thence north-easterly along said centre line to the point at which the same is intersected by the centre line of Kinnamox or Quinamass Bay, thence in a straight line to the point of commencement.

❧

In view of all that has been hereinbefore stated Your Petitioners, claiming to hold a tribal title to the whole of the said territory both by aboriginal right and under the said Proclamation, and having no other recourse for securing justice, humbly place this Petition before Your Majesty as the source and fountain of all justice, having supreme authority over all persons and matters within Your Majesty's dominions, and possessing and exercising upon and with the advice of Your Majesty's Privy Council original judicial jurisdiction.

❧

Your Petitioners most humbly pray that Your Majesty in Council may be pleased to take into Your Most Gracious Consideration the matters hereinbefore set forth, and in exercise of the original jurisdiction to which reference has above been made and all other jurisdiction relating to such matters possessed by Your Majesty in Council and upon report made to Your Majesty in Council by a Committee of the whole of Your Majesty Privy Council, or upon report so made by the Judicial Committee or other Committee of the Council to which Your Majesty in Council may see fit to refer the same, may adjudge such matters and determine all question arising therefrom for decision.

❧

This Petition is presented by the Nishga Nation or Tribe of Indians through their Agents, Messrs. Fox and Preece, of 15, Dean's Yard, Westminster, Solicitors, in pursuance of a resolution passed at a meeting of the said Nishga Nation or Tribe, held at the Village of Kincolith situated on the Nass River in the Province of British Columbia, on Wednesday, the 22nd day of January, 1913.

*All Nisga'a names, common spelling at the time Note: Excerpted from Petition to His Majesty's Privy Council, lodged on 21st May, 1913

Nisga'a Land Committee, 1913

(From left to right)

4th Row:

Charlie Elliot, Mark Smith, Brian Peal, Charlie Brown, William Stevens

3rd Row:

Matthew Russ, Jeremiah Clayton, Charlie Davis, Leonard Douglas, Benjamin Benson, George Pollard

2nd Row:

Benjamin Monroe, Peter Calder, William Lincoln, George Woodfield, Lazarus Moody, Andrew Mercer,

William Angus, Alfred McKay, George Eli, Johnny Moore

1st Row:

Paul Mercer, John Wesley, Steven Allan, Arthur Calder, Charlie Barton, William Foster,

Sam Pollard, William McNeil

The Nisga'a Tribal Council was formed in 1955, uniting the four Nisga'a clans (Eagle, Wolf, Raven and Killer Whale) and their communities (Gingolx, Lakalzap, Gitwinksihlkw and Gitlakdamiks). By working to settle the Land Question, the council ultimately caused a fundamental shift in federal policy concerning aboriginal title in non-treaty areas of Canada. Incorporating itself in 1963 under the provincial Societies Act, the council has been served by three past presidents.

FRANK CALDER
President 1957-1973

"The Nisga'a Land Question will be settled. Of that we are certain.
We are prepared to do whatever is necessary to bring this about."

HLEEḴ
JAMES GOSNELL
President 1973-1988

"We are willing to share, and have said so hundreds of times. We want a treaty that will finally
recognize your laws and system of government and, in return, you will recognize ours."

SIM'OOGIT DAAX̱HEET
ALVIN McKAY
President 1988-1993

"After decades of indifference to the demands of aboriginal peoples, Canadians have accepted
the notion that we have the inherent right to self-government."

Nisga'a Tribal Council, 1993

(From left to right)

3rd Row:

Collier Azak, Martin Adams, Henry Moore, Tommy Dennis, Perry Azak, Herbert Morven, Harry Nyce

2nd Row:

John A. MacKenzie, Max McNeil, Charles McKay, Stuart Doolan, Ben Stewart, Daisy Clayton, Steve Azak

1st Row:

Rod Robinson, Edmond Wright, Joseph Gosnell Sr., Kevin McKay, Kathleen Clayton, Frank Calder

Missing:

Hubert Barton, Nelson Leeson

1763 – The Royal Proclamation, issued in the name of King George III, excludes all settlement from and restricts all trade on Indian lands.

1774 – Spanish Captain Juan Francisco de la Bodega y Quadra sails near the Nass River.

1790 – Sea otter fur trade begins.

1793 – The Captain Vancouver expedition to Observatory Inlet and Salmon Cove produces first contact between the Nisga'a and explorers.

1831 – Peter Skene Ogden supervises construction of Fort Nass for the Hudson's Bay Company.

1836 – Smallpox epidemic devastates Indians of the Northwest coast.

1858 – The Colony of British Columbia is established.

1862 – Second wave of smallpox. About 20,000 of B.C.'s 60,000 Indians die.

1864 – Joseph Trutch appointed B.C. Commissioner of Lands and Works.

1876 – Federal government agrees not to discuss aboriginal title before establishing reserves.

1878 – Federal government begins interfering with Indian fishing rights.

1886 – The Nisga'a in the Upper Nass send government surveyors packing. Nisga'a chiefs lobby Victoria on the Land Question.

1889 – Federal fishing permit system introduced.

1890 – Nisga'a establish their Land Committee, the first of its kind in Canada.

1909 – The Nisga'a Land Committee and other northcoast tribes form the Native Tribes of B.C.

1910 – Prime Minister Laurier in Prince Rupert promises to settle the Land Question.

1913 – Nisga'a send a petition to British Privy Council to resolve the Land Question.

1923 – Natives allowed to become commercial fishermen.

1924 – The McKenna-McBride Commission allots 76 square kilometres of reserve land to Nisga'a.

1927 – Federal government prohibits natives from organizing to discuss land claims.

1931 – Native Brotherhood of B.C. is formed and secretly keeps Land Question discussions alive.

1955 – The Nisga'a Land Committee is re-established as the Nisga'a Tribal Council.

1961 – Natives gain vote in federal elections.

1968 – Nisga'a take the Land Question to court.

1973 – Supreme Court of Canada splits on question of aboriginal title.

1976 – Negotiations to settle Land Question begin with provincial and federal governments.

1982 – The Constitution of Canada recognizes and affirms aboriginal rights.

1991 – B.C. government agrees to enter negotiations with Nisga'a.

1991 – B.C. government recognizes aboriginal title and inherent right to self-government.